BIBLE

Patricia Perry

BARBOUR
PUBLISHING, INC.
Uhrichsville, Ohio

© MCMXCVIII by Barbour Publishing, Inc.

ISBN 1-57748-439-8

All rights reserved. No part of this publication may be reproduced or transmitted in any form or by any means without written permission of the publisher.

Published by Barbour Publishing, Inc.,
P.O. Box 719, Uhrichsville, Ohio 44683
http://www.barbourbooks.com

Printed in the United States of America.

Welcome to your Bible! God wrote this special book just for you. Inside the Bible you will find God's wonderful plan for each of us. Every page tells us more about who God is and about His love and forgiveness. It's an exciting book!

There are many different titles for the Bible. Some titles are: *The Holy Bible, The Good News Bible,* or *The Book.* Your Bible may have a different title. Look at the cover of your Bible. What is the name on it?

Write the title here:

_____

"Hello!"
"How are you?"
"WHAT'S HAPPENING?"
"Hi!"
"HOW'S IT GOING?"
"Hey dude!"

All of these are different ways of greeting someone. You and your friends may have your own special greeting that means hello.

Write down your way of saying "hello" here:

_____

The Bible was first written in three different languages: Hebrew, Greek and Aramaic. People worked hard to translate the Bible into English. They tried to be as accurate as possible. Still, different translators may say the same thing in many different ways. These different ways are called *versions*.

What version is your Bible? Sometimes it says on the cover, sometimes you have to look inside on the first few pages.

On the lines below write the version of the Bible you have:

_____

_____

INSPIRATION

The Bible is the Word of God. Even though men wrote the words down, God told them what He wanted them to say. We call that "inspiration."

God wanted them to write down his message so that He could tell you how much He loves you. That's right! The Bible is the story of God's love for us from the beginning of time.

He shows us his love in the stories and in songs and in his teaching.

Try the following challenge. To solve this puzzle you must first fill in the blanks in the following statements.

1. I like to throw and catch a
   _____.

2. My dog has a wagging
   _____.

3. The month after April is
   _____.

4. When I know the answer in
   class I raise my
   _____.

Now circle the first letter of each of the words you wrote. Using your pencil, black out each of those letters in the puzzle below. When you are finished, you will know what the Bible is all about!

```
B  L  M  H
G  O  D'  S
B  V  T  H
H  E  T  M
```

Now look in the index in the front pages of your Bible. You will see that the Bible is really a collection of smaller books.

The first five books were written down by Moses. We call them the Books of the Law. The Ten Commandments are in those books as well as many exciting stories about God and His people.

Other books are books of history, poetry, and prophecy. You will also see that the Bible is divided into the Old Testament and the New Testament.

> Count the number of books in the Old Testament: _____
> Count the number of books in the New Testament: _____
> Now add the total number of books in the Bible: _____

The Old Testament books tell us about the creation of the earth, sun, moon and stars. We learn of Adam and Eve in the Garden of Eden and about God's love for his people.

The New Testament books tell us about Jesus' birth in a stable in Bethlehem, about his life, his teaching, his death and resurrection. We find out about the early church and how the Good News of Jesus spread to all the people.

The books are arranged in the same order in every Bible. If you get used to the order of books or memorize them (it's easier than it looks) you will be able to find any book quickly and easily. Let's try it. What is the name of the very first book of the Old Testament?

Write the title here:

_____

OLD TESTAMENT WORD FIND

Read over the list of names of the books of the Old Testament, then try this puzzle:

ALL of the books of the OLD TESTAMENT are in the word find on the next page. Books that have two parts are listed once (Samuel, Kings, and Chronicles) so that you will find a total of 36 different titles. Song of Solomon is listed here as Song of Songs. Use your Bible's index for a list of all the books.

Words may be across, down, upside down, or backwards. There are no diagonals.

```
P S Q G E N E S I S D J O N A H
S G W C L E I K E Z E M U H A N
A N E H S B O J L E U M A S Y Z
L I Z R N X Z O A P T P V J E E
M K R O O Z X S M H E R S O C C
S D A N I E L H O A R O R E C H
L E V I T I C U S N O V E L L A
J Q J C A G P A X I N E B W E R
E M U L T R U T H A O R M H S I
R A D E N M I C A H M B U A I A
E L G S E S T H E R Y S N I A H
M A E Q M Q X E X O D U S D S O
I C S H A B A K K U K L L A T S
A H Y G L H A G G A I W Q B E E
H I M M S G N O S F O G N O S A
N E H E M I A H X I S A I A H Q
```

When you mail a letter the address on the envelope tells the post office the state, city, street, and house number.

The Bible address system works in a similar way. We can easily find any verse in the Bible. A verse is a sentence or a short phrase.

First we say the name of the book, then what chapter it is in, and finally the verse number.

It is written like this:

Book chapter:verse

The very first verse in the Bible is Genesis 1:1. Say, "the book of

Genesis, chapter 1, verse 1."

- See if you can find it.
- Turn to the book of Genesis. (It is the first book of the Bible.)
- Now turn to the first chapter.
- Finally, look at the first verse.
- Write the first verse of the Bible here:

_____

_____

_____

_____

_____

_____

You can find any verse of the Bible this way. As you turn the pages, look at the top of each page. You will see that the title of the book, the chapter, and the verse that you will find on these pages are listed at the top right and at the top left. It works just like a dictionary. Now try your skill in the next game.

BATTING 1,000

Total your answers to the following questions. If you are correct, your total should be 1,000!

1. Adam was the first man. Turn to Genesis 5:5 to find out how old he was when he died.

    Answer _____

2. How many people entered Noah's ark to escape the great flood? Look at Genesis 7:13.

   Answer _____

3. Before the tower of Babel, how many different languages were in the world? Genesis 11:1

   Answer _____

4. How many brothers did Joseph have? Genesis 37:9. Hint: He saw his brothers as stars in a dream.

   Answer _____

5. How many chapters are there in the book of Genesis?

   Answer _____

Now total your answers: _____

If you hit 1,000,
you are the champion!

Now that you know how the Bible Address System works, you can find any verse you want.

Look at the second book of the Bible, Exodus.

Now look up Exodus 2:10.
What was the name of the baby that Pharaoh's daughter found floating in a basket?

_____

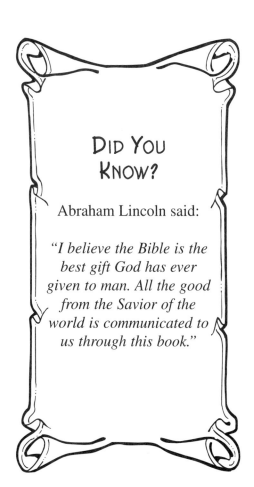

Did You Know?

Abraham Lincoln said:

"I believe the Bible is the best gift God has ever given to man. All the good from the Savior of the world is communicated to us through this book."

One of the favorite books in the Old Testament is the book of Psalms. Most books are stories of God and His people. But the book of Psalms is actually a book of songs.

If you open your Bible to about the middle, you will find the book of Psalms. (Hint: if you don't find it right away turn forward or back a few pages at a time.)

- Find the book of Psalms now.
- See how each Psalm is numbered?

There are 150 Psalms. Most of them

were written by David. You may have heard of the story of David and Goliath. David was a warrior, but he was also a musician and a song writer.

Find Psalm 23. It is the best known of all the Psalms and tells of God being like a shepherd taking care of his sheep.

As you read Psalm 23, you may have noticed little numbers next to some words. These numbers help us find the exact phrase or verse we want to study.

How many verses are there in Psalm 23?

Answer _____

Which verse tells us that God, our Lord, is like a shepherd?

Answer _____

Look at verse four. Why do you never need to be afraid?

Answer _____

_____

_____

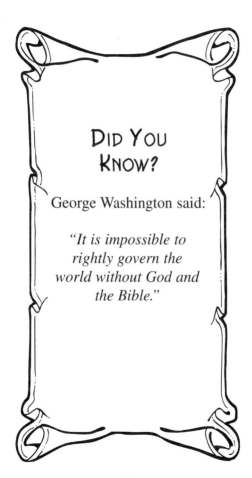

DID YOU KNOW?

George Washington said:

"It is impossible to rightly govern the world without God and the Bible."

PROVERBS

Turn to Proverbs, the book that comes after Psalms. Remember that Psalms is in the center of your Bible. Solve the coded puzzle below to find out what you can have by reading this book.

$\overline{} \ \overline{} \ \overline{}$
 4   8   1

$\overline{} \ \overline{} \ \overline{} \ \overline{} \ \overline{} \ \overline{}$
 6 13 5 11 2 10

$\overline{} \; \overline{} \quad \overline{} \; \overline{} \; \overline{} \; \overline{}$
2 7   3 13 9 12

$\overline{} \; \overline{} \; \overline{} \; \overline{} \; \overline{} \; \overline{} \; \overline{}$
5 2 14 2 10 2 9

KEY

1 = E   6 = W   11 = D

2 = O   7 = F   12 = G

3 = K   8 = H   13 = I

4 = T   9 = N   14 = L

5 = S   10 = M

You may remember that the Bible is divided into two sections: the *Old Testament* and the *New Testament.*

The Old Testament talks about time from creation until the birth of Jesus.

The New Testament tells about Jesus' birth and life, the first Christians, and that Jesus is coming again someday!

Find the New Testament in your Bible. It is about two-thirds back.

Write the name of the first book of the New Testament here:

_____

Did You Know?

That the Bible was written by forty different authors, over 1,600 years, and yet it all has the same theme? Imagine if just six students in your class, without speaking to each other, each tried to write a part of the same story. How do you think the story would turn out?

New Testament Word Find

Just like the Old Testament, the books of the New Testament are in the same order in every Bible. You will find a list of New Testament books either at the beginning of the New Testament in your Bible, or at the front of your Bible before the Old Testament books.

See if you can find all the books of the New Testament. Books with a I, II, or III in front of them are only listed once so there are a total of 21 titles to look for.

```
T R E V E L A T I O N S S
H E B R E W S J U D E R T
E P H E S I A N S J O O C
S E T I J O H N M A Q M O
S T I M O T H Y A M V A R
A E T Q H P R W R E N N I
L R U O N T R W K S L S N
O J S A C T S L U K E V T
N U G A L A T I A N S M H
I D M A T T H E W L K L I
A C O L O S S I A N S Q A
N P H I L E M O N V B Z N
S K P H I L I P P I A N S
```

The first four books of the New Testament are called the *Gospels*. That means *The Good News*. The Gospels tell about Jesus' life. The Gospels were written by men named Matthew, Mark, Luke, and John.

You will notice that many of the books of the Bible have loo-oo-oo-ng names. To make it easier, we shorten, or abbreviate, those names. Watch out for abbreviations and for different books in the next puzzle!

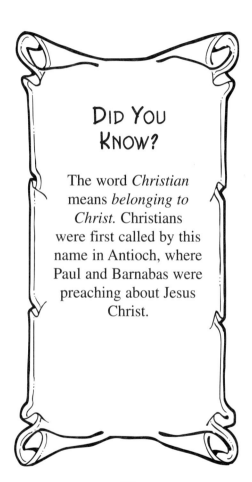

Did You Know?

The word *Christian* means *belonging to Christ.* Christians were first called by this name in Antioch, where Paul and Barnabas were preaching about Jesus Christ.

ALL 'A'S AND ONE 'B'

The first letter to each answer will start with the letter 'A' except one. It will start with the letter 'B'.

1. Who appeared to Joseph in a dream?

    MATT. 1:20

    _____

2. The first two apostles (followers of Jesus) were Simon Peter and his brother.

    MATT. 4:18

    _____

3. Jesus said that we should seek, knock and _____.

   MATT. 7:7

4. Even though Jesus never did anything wrong, soldiers came to _____ him.

   MARK 14:46

5. After Jesus rose from his death, He came to be with the apostles and _____ some fish with them.

   LUKE 24:43

6. These things, in the Bible, are written so that you may _____ in Jesus Christ.

   JOHN 20:31

The Book of *Acts* tells what happened when Jesus went to heaven and how Christianity spread to all the world. The *Epistles* are *letters* that the apostles wrote to the new Christians. They help us to understand more about living the Christian life.

Many of the letters were written by Paul. He traveled by ship and on foot and had many exciting adventures telling people about Jesus.

In the puzzle below, x out all the 'q's to find out what Paul wrote to the people of Rome in the book of Romans.

QIQ QTQHAQNKQ GQODQ FQOQR YQOQU QAQLQL QANQDQ QREQMEQMBQER QYOQUQQ QIQNQ QMQYQ PQRQAQYQEQRS.

Answer:

_____

_____

_____

_____

_____

_____

_____

REVELATION

The book of *Revelation* tells about Jesus' return. It is an exciting book of *prophecy*. Prophecy means to tell what God says today and also can mean telling what will happen in the future. Only God's prophecies are 100% accurate.

In the Old Testament there are many books that told of Jesus coming to earth as a man to pay for our sins. Revelation tells of Jesus' final return to rule the earth.

Several pages ago you wrote down the first verse in the Bible. Now turn to Revelation 22:20–21. What are the last words that Jesus gives us?

_____

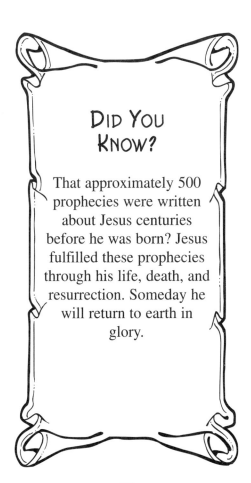

Did You Know?

That approximately 500 prophecies were written about Jesus centuries before he was born? Jesus fulfilled these prophecies through his life, death, and resurrection. Someday he will return to earth in glory.

GOD'S FAMILY

Do you want to be a member of God's family? Over and over in the Bible, God tells us that He loves us and wants us to be with Him.

But something keeps us apart. That thing is called "sin."

Sin is anything that points us away from God, instead of toward Him. Everyone has sinned, or gone their own way instead of God's way.

The only one who could take care of the sin problem is Jesus. That is why he came to earth and died for our sins.

When you eat dinner "out" with your parents, they pay the bill for the food you eat. They love you and want you to be with them. All you have to do is eat!

Jesus paid the bill for our sins when he died on the cross for us. All *you* have to do is accept his forgiveness and ask Him to be with you forever!

Jesus didn't stay dead. He arose from the dead by his own power. He gives us the gift of eternal life. When we accept his forgiveness and ask him into our hearts, we become spiritually alive. Our bodies may someday die, but our spirits will live forever with Him in heaven.

PRAYER

How can you be forgiven and have eternal life with Jesus?

All you have to do is pray a simple prayer. Prayer is talking to God. He can hear you and knows your thoughts. You need to pray with faith, that is, really mean what you say and believe that God is here, listening to you.

Say this prayer now:

Jesus,

I know that you died on the cross for my sins. Thank you for forgiving me and for the gift of eternal life.

Please, be with me, now and always. Amen.

If you have prayed this prayer, write today's date here:

_____

This is your new spiritual birthday!

Jesus promises that once you ask him to be with you, he will never leave you—no matter what you do, no matter what you say. Jesus is not a sometimes friend. He is an all times friend.

Now that you are a Christian, you are a member of God's family. Pray to Him every day. Read your Bible, too. Try reading one of the Gospels or a Psalm. This is God's Word to you. Attend church or Sunday school and make Christian friends.

Welcome

Benvenuto

WILLKOMMEN

BIENVENIDO

Welkom

BIENVENUE

Bem-vindo

WELCOME TO GOD'S FAMILY!

Answers

Page 7
If you found *God's Love* you were right!

Page 8
There are *39* books in the Old Testament and *27* books in the New Testament for a total of *66* books in the Bible.

Page 9
If you said *Genesis* you were right!
   The word "Genesis" means "beginning."

Page 11

PAGE 13

The 1st verse tells us that *God made heaven and earth.*

PAGES 14–15
1. Adam lived to be *930*.
2. There were *eight* people in the ark: Noah, Mrs. Noah, their three sons and their wives.
3. There was only *one* language.
4. Joseph had *eleven* brothers.
5. There are *fifty* chapters in the book of Genesis.

PAGE 16

Yes! The answer is *Moses*.

You may want to read the whole story of Moses located in the book of Exodus.

PAGES 19–20
There are *six* verses in Psalm 23.
Verse one tells us God is like a loving shepherd.
We don't ever have to be afraid because *God is always with us.*

PAGES 22–23
Yes! You can have:
The Wisdom of King Solomon.

PAGE 24
Matthew is the first book of the New Testament.

Page 27

```
T  R  E  V  E  L  A  T  I  O  N  S  S
H  E  B  R  E  W  S  J  U  D  E  R  T
E  P  H  E  S  I  A  N  S  J  O  O  C
S  E  T  I  J  O  H  N  M  A  Q  M  O
S  T  I  M  O  T  H  Y  A  M  V  A  R
A  E  T  Q  H  P  R  W  R  E  N  N  I
L  R  U  O  N  T  R  W  K  S  L  S  N
O  J  S  A  C  T  S  L  U  K  E  V  T
N  U  G  A  L  A  T  I  A  N  S  M  H
I  D  M  A  T  T  H  E  W  L  K  L  I
A  C  O  L  O  S  S  I  A  N  S  Q  A
N  P  H  I  L  E  M  O  N  V  B  Z  N
S  K  P  H  I  L  I  P  P  I  A  N  S
```

PAGES 30–31
Did you find them all?
1. Angel
2. Andrew
3. Ask
4. Arrest
5. Ate
6. Believe

PAGE 33
Paul wrote:
> *I thank God for you all and remember you in my prayers.*

PAGE 34
Yes! *He is coming soon!*

Hey, kids—
There's more fun in the Little Library series!

Enjoy jokes, trivia, and puzzles? Then look for these other great Little Library books—they're the right price, a great size, and packed with fun!

Great Clean Jokes Lots of good, clean fun—a bonanza of jokes you can share with anyone!
99 cents

Fun Bible Trivia Questions and answers from the Bible—test your Bible IQ!   99 cents

Bible Word Search Collection No. 1 How sharp are your eyes? Can you find the Bible words hidden in each puzzle?   99 cents

Available wherever books are sold.
Or order from:

Barbour Publishing, Inc.
P.O. Box 719
Uhrichsville, OH 44683
http://www.barbourbooks.com

If you order by mail,
add $2.00 to your order for shipping.
Prices subject to change without notice.